Human Trafficking in Texas

More Resources and Resolve Needed to Stem Surge of Modern Day Slavery

A Report of the Texas Advisory Committee to the
United States Commission on Civil Rights

August 2011

State Advisory Committees to the United States Commission on Civil Rights

By law, the U.S. Commission on Civil Rights has established an advisory committee in each of the 50 states and the District of Columbia. The committees are composed of state citizens who serve without compensation. State Advisory Committees advise the Commission concerning civil rights issues in their states that are within the Commission's jurisdiction. More specifically, they are authorized to advise the Commission on matters of their state's concern in the preparation of Commission reports to the President and the Congress; receive reports, suggestions, and recommendations from individuals, public officials, and representatives of public and private organizations to committee inquiries; forward advice and recommendations to the Commission, as requested; and observe any open hearing or conference conducted by the Commission in their states.

Texas Advisory Committee to the U.S. Commission on Civil Rights

Merrill Matthews, *Chairman*
Coppell

Charles Z. Burchett Kirbyville	Bill Calhoun Houston
Frances A. Carnot** San Antonio	Jason P. Casellas Austin
Russell B. Casey Hurst	Cecilia R. Castillo San Marcos
Glenn O. Lewis Fort Worth	Cathy McConn Houston
Harriet Miller Dallas	Martha Orozco Houston
Charles E. Stolfus** Denton	Barbara J. Walters** Plano

** Members of the Texas Advisory Committee sub-Committee on Human Trafficking

Letter of Transmittal

**Texas Advisory Committee to the
U.S. Commission on Civil Rights**

Kimberly L. Tolhurst, *Delegated the Authority of the Staff Director*

The Texas Advisory Committee to the U.S. Commission on Civil Rights submits this report, *Human Trafficking in Texas—More Resources and Resolve Needed to Stem Surge in Modern Day Slavery,* as part of its responsibility to examine and report on civil rights issues under the jurisdiction of the Commission. This report is the unanimous statement by all members of the Texas Committee and is approved by a vote of 13 yes and 0 no.

Human trafficking is the cruel and vicious practice of transporting human beings for the purpose of labor or sex exploitation. At its core it is a violation of the fundamental civil rights of its victims. Women are the overwhelming victims of human trafficking, and victims generally come from impoverished circumstances with the majority being from indigenous populations or ethnic minorities.

The trafficking of humans is a growing problem in this country, and Texas—as one of the largest border states in the United States—is considered a major destination and transit state for human trafficking.

Human trafficking is a high-profit and relatively low-risk business with ample supply and growing demand. Every year, it is estimated that one million to two million persons world-wide are victims of human trafficking. In 2010, for the first time, the United States was ranked in the State Department's annual *Trafficking in Persons Report* that documents human trafficking and modern slavery. The report found that in America, men, women, and children were subject to trafficking for "forced labor, debt bondage, and forced prostitution."

Tragically, despite the shocking statistics and the inherent brutality of human trafficking, it is a crime that still has not captured the attention of the public nor made it to the top of political agendas. Few cases ever make it to the courts, and in a cruel irony it is often the victim rather than the perpetrator who is prosecuted for an illegal activity. There continues to be limited resources for law enforcement, and few resources devoted to rehabilitating its victims.

Apart from the obvious civil rights violations of the victims, it needs to be emphasized that human trafficking—like all civil rights violations—also has a pernicious effect on the larger community. Human trafficking erodes the fabric of the society; has a negative effect on the economy; stresses the local tax base; and puts added pressure on border enforcement and national security.

In issuing this report the Texas Advisory Committee seeks to bring attention to the pernicious problem of human trafficking; the limited resources devoted to combating this problem; and the likely long-term high social costs for the general society if this civil rights issue is not addressed.

Respectfully,

Merrill Matthews, *Chairman*
Texas State Advisory Committee

Table of Contents

HUMAN TRAFFICKING DEFINED

Human trafficking is the coercion of human beings for the purpose of forced labor, sexual exploitation, or both.[1] It is a cruel, vicious practice which violates the victim's fundamental civil rights. Overwhelmingly, women are the victims of human trafficking.

This criminal activity is very profitable. One estimate is that human trafficking generates $32 billion in annual profits for the perpetrators.[2] Generally, victims come from impoverished circumstances, with the majority being from indigenous populations or ethnic minorities. Typically, the victims live in circumstances where there are few viable economic alternatives, and effective social structures often do not exist to protect would-be victims.[3]

> *Sex trafficking:* the procurement of persons for commercial sex induced by force or coercion.

A common denominator of human trafficking is the use of force or coercion to exploit a person for profit. The U.S. State Department categorizes human trafficking under two general major classes, sex trafficking and involuntary servitude.[4]

● *Sex trafficking:*
the procurement and use of persons for commercial sex that is induced by force or coercion.

● *Involuntary servitude:*
the impressment of persons for labor services, most of whom are harbored in confining conditions or as actual slaves.

Worldwide, an estimated 27 million persons are in bondage, meaning they are being forced into commercial sex acts or confined in involuntary servitude.[5]

Each year as many as 800,000 persons are trafficked across international borders. This figure does not include the thousands of persons who are trafficked within their own countries.[6] Despite these large numbers, few purveyors of human trafficking are brought to justice.

> *Involuntary servitude:* the impressment of persons for labor services, most victims being confined as actual slaves.

Human trafficking has emerged as a major civil rights issue of the 21st century. Despite the shocking statistics and the brutality of human trafficking, it is a crime that still has not captured the attention of the public nor made it to the top of political agendas.

More than 15 years ago, there was burgeoning attention to this problem as a civil rights violation. As females are the large majority of victims, early reports on the issue urged a renewed focus on the elimination of sex-based violence in order to enhance the civil and human rights of women and girls.[7]

In issuing this report the Texas Advisory Committee to the U.S. Commission on Civil Rights seeks to bring attention to the existence of this important civil rights issue and the potential long-term social costs if this problem is not addressed.

Social Costs and the Magnitude of Human Trafficking

An anti-trafficking hotline receives a frantic call from a woman who says she has been kept in a brothel and said she was afraid the brothel operators would hurt her family in her home country if she did not prostitute. The caller says the brothel is next to a migrant labor community and the women in the brothel are afraid of being deported.[8]

The above story is a real example of human trafficking for sex in the United States. In 2010, for the first time, the United States was listed in the State Department's annual *Trafficking in Persons Report,* which recounted occurrences of human trafficking and modern slavery in America. The report found that throughout the United States, men, women, and children were subject to trafficking for "forced labor, debt bondage, and forced prostitution."[9]

Human Trafficking Erodes Family Structure

Victims of human trafficking suffer extreme physical and mental abuse as well as social stigmatization. Victims of human trafficking have their psyches destroyed and lose their sense of dignity and self worth. They become isolated, losing ties with their former lives and families. The ability of victims to have long-term nurturing relationships is compromised. Unchecked, this growing group of traumatized persons can undermine society's ability to have intact, stable families.

Exacerbating the problem is the realization that human trafficking does not take place in a vacuum. Many social ills such as poverty, homelessness, and broken homes play a role in allowing human trafficking to exist and thrive. These social conditions produce the environments in which the vulnerable become prey and perpetrators and patrons alike often act with impunity.

Females who are most vulnerable to being trafficked are those aged 10-35 and who are impoverished, poorly educated, or from indigenous, ethnic minority, rural or refugee groups. Such females often lack access to education and meaningful employment opportunities.

Human Trafficking Raises Social and Public Health Costs

At the societal level, human trafficking undermines development efforts and raises social and health costs. Besides the obvious human violations against its victims, human trafficking also has a negative effect on the economy. The estimated cost of forced labor is over $20 billion in the form of lost income due to unpaid wages. This exploitation undermines not only the ability of victims to economically support families, but increases social costs to the general society to provide health care and other essential services.[10]

In addition, human trafficking hinders the educational development and the productive potential of the victims, especially children and teenagers. It also negatively affects the victims' physical and psychological health, as they are sometimes excluded from society due to the trauma of their experiences of exploitation.[11]

Human Trafficking Puts Additional Pressure on Border Security

Human trafficking is a high-profit and relatively low-risk business with ample supply and growing demand. Every year, it is estimated that worldwide one to two million men, women, and children become victims of human trafficking.

Here in the United States, Texas is considered a major destination for victims of human trafficking. According to statistics, in 2008, 38 percent of all calls to the National Trafficking Resource Center hot line were dialed in Texas. Between 2001 and 2006, the total number of persons prosecuted for human trafficking in the United States tripled. In the same period, the number of persons prosecuted for sex slavery increased four times.[12]

Traffickers of persons into this country can make between $13,000 and $67,000 per person trafficked.[13] As a victim's illegal status makes it difficult for them to seek help from law enforcement, high profits prompt an increasingly larger number of profiteers to bring victims across this Nation's borders straining an already overwhelmed border protection service.

Magnitude of the Problem

In recent years, the U.S. State Department has reported that as many as 20,000 persons may be trafficked annually into the United States. Victims reportedly are brought into this country from all parts of the world.
- 5,000-7,000 come into the U.S. from East Asia and the Pacific;
- 3,500-5,500 come into the U.S. from Latin America; and
- 7,000-11,000 come into the U.S. from Europe and Eurasia.[14]

Sex trafficking is the predominant form of human trafficking in the United States, and accounts for 83 percent of all reported incidents. Twelve percent of all domestic cases involve labor trafficking, while 5 percent are other forms of trafficking.[14]

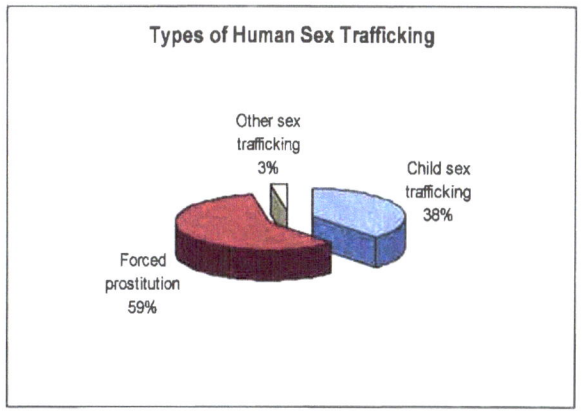

Source: U.S. Department of Justice.

Forced prostitution (46 percent) and child sex trafficking (30 percent) represent the two largest categories of confirmed sex trafficking incidents. Of the more than 1,000 alleged sex trafficking incidents reported by task forces, 38 percent involved allegations of child sex trafficking and 62 percent of all incidents involved allegations of adult sex trafficking, such as forced prostitution or other sex trafficking crimes.[15]

Migrant smuggling, which is the illegal transportation of undocumented persons into the United States, should not be confused with human trafficking. Migrant smuggling occurs with the consent of the person(s) being smuggled. Victims of human trafficking are illegally brought into the country and are prevented from leaving their confinement by physical or psychological coercion as well as legal and financial constraints.

WHERE HUMAN TRAFFICKING IS HAPPENING IN TEXAS

As a state with one of the largest borders in the country, Texas is widely considered a major destination and transit state for human trafficking. Interstate 10 (image below) is the major east-west Interstate Highway in the southern part of the United States. In Texas, this interstate links three major urban areas: El Paso, San Antonio, and Houston.

Interstate 10 runs east from El Paso near the border with New Mexico, connecting with San Antonio in the south-central part of the state, and continuing onto Houston near the border of Louisiana. The length of Interstate 10 crossing Texas is the longest continuous un-tolled freeway under a single authority in North America.

Figure 1
Interstate 10 in Texas

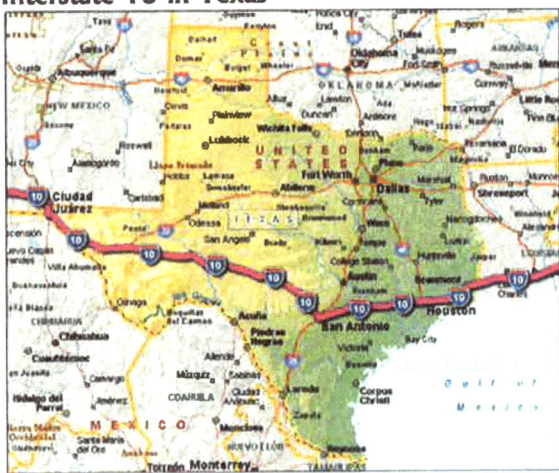

At the 2006 Department of Justice National Conference on Human Trafficking, the interstate I-10 corridor was identified as one of the main routes for human traffickers. Two cities along the I-10 corridor figure prominently as centers identified with a particularly high level of human trafficking: El Paso and Houston. [16]

The U.S. Department of Justice's report on activities to combat human trafficking identified El Paso and Houston on its list of "most intense trafficking jurisdictions in the country." The second largest trafficking bust in U.S. history occurred in Houston. More than 90 victims were rescued during the raid by law enforcement officials and referred to local service providers to assist them in their recovery process. [17]

> *"It's hard for me to believe how the biggest free country in the world can have the most slaves in the world."*
> *Local Texas Investigator*

State and federal authorities and social services providers working with human trafficking victims in Texas find it difficult to quantify the extent of human trafficking. Currently Texas law does not require law enforcement agencies or the courts to compile and report statistics specific to human trafficking cases. It is therefore impossible to know with any degree of certainty the extent of the problem. [1]

Statistical analysis is further made difficult because traffickers may be charged with other violations, such as kidnapping or sexual assault, in lieu of a human trafficking charge. Others often accept plea bargains with lesser penalties. Still, the number of cases reported show sharp increases in prosecution of human trafficking in Texas locations where data is being reported. [18]

---

[1] Under the TVPA, the federal government provides funding to local communities to develop task forces to combat human trafficking. Only federally funded Human Trafficking Task Forces are required to maintain and report data on human trafficking.

CURRENT AND PROSPECTIVE LAWS IN TEXAS

Federal, state and local law enforcement agencies all have specific roles in the effort to combat human trafficking. At the national level, the federal government is responsible for ensuring the sovereignty of the borders and investigating criminal activity that crosses state lines and/or violates federal statutes. At the state and local level, law enforcement agencies have the responsibility to police and prosecute local criminal activity.

A perception exists that only foreign nationals are victims of human trafficking in the United States. Arrest and prosecution records show that to be false; significant incidents of domestic human trafficking occur within Texas in addition to movement of victims through Texas to other states.

At the federal level, the Trafficking Victims Protection Act (TVPA) provides $95 million in assistance to local law enforcement agencies to enforce the anti-trafficking provisions of the law.[19] The federal law includes severe punishments—including life imprisonment, for persons who are convicted of operating trafficking enterprises within the United States. The law was amended in 2008, in part to better track statistics. The amended act orders the Federal Bureau of Investigation to present more detail on human trafficking, and to break down the categories of prostitution and commercialized sex act vice arrests in the Uniform Crime Reports.[20]

Texas introduced a state human trafficking law in 2003, making Washington and Texas the first two states in the nation to enact laws that criminalized human trafficking. The act established criminal definitions for "forced labor or services" and "trafficking," and set out offenses and penalties for persons convicted of human trafficking offenses. In addition to actual trafficking, illegal activity under the act was expanded to encompass enticing, recruiting, harboring, or otherwise obtaining a person by any means.[21]

In 2007, the Texas Legislature passed legislation that required the State of Texas Office of the Attorney General (OAG), in consultation with the state's Health and Human Services Commission (HHSC), to prepare a report detailing how existing laws and rules governing victims and witnesses address–or fails to address–the needs of victims. The report recommended changes to existing laws and rules to enhance the ability of law enforcement to prosecute traffickers for criminal conduct.[22]

> **Texas introduced a human trafficking law in 2003 making it one of the first two states to criminalize human trafficking.**

Recent legislation passed by the Texas Legislature is designed to enhance the state's ability to combat domestic human trafficking. The legislation added offenses for benefitting from forced labor and services, changing the age of a minor victim from under 14 years of age to under 18 years of age. It also requires the posting notices of the national human trafficking hotline in overnight lodging establishments that had been deemed a nuisance due to premise activities.[23]

5

As awareness of human trafficking in the state increased, it was recognized that a need existed for additional training and collaboration among law enforcement agencies. In response, legislation was enacted in 2009 created the Texas Human Trafficking Prevention Task Force. A primary purpose for the task force is to coordinate a statewide response to human trafficking.[24]

The task force is authorized for four years, and is required to make annual reports to the Legislature. Its responsibilities also include:

- increase collaboration among multi-jurisdictional law enforcement agencies and non-governmental organizations;
- collect and publish data on the extent of human trafficking in Texas;
- develop and conduct training for victim service providers, law enforcement, the judiciary, court personnel, and medical service providers;
- implement media awareness campaign;
- develop policies and procedures that will prevent and help prosecute human trafficking.[25]

> **"Texas needs to develop a sustainable plan for the long term viability of its war on human trafficking."**
> **--Texas Human Trafficking Task Force**

The Texas Human Trafficking Prevention Task Force submitted its second Report to the Texas Legislature in January 2011. It cited progress, but observed: "Texas needs to develop a sustainable plan to continue the long term viability of its war on human trafficking." The task force also set forth a series of recommendations, including additional protections for victims.[26]

The legislative priorities and initiatives the Texas Human Trafficking Task Force recommends are summarized below, and can be found in more detail in the Report:

- Identify Prevention Strategies -- *reduce risk factors, increase training and outreach, identify additional deterrents*
- Increase Victim Identification and Offender Prosecutions -- *increase prosecution of traffickers, improve collaboration and response area, create a network of services and a centralized repository for information*
- Provide Protection for Adult Human Trafficking Victims -- *find funding for victim services*[2]
- Provide Protection for Child Human Trafficking Victims -- *develop comprehensive services for victims and enhance penalties for criminals*
- Improve Awareness and Education to Increase Detection
- Improve Data Collection
- Develop more Intelligence-sharing Among Law Enforcement Agencies

As noted in the task force report, victims of human sex trafficking are often prosecuted as criminals. This includes children under the age of 18. As Jennifer Solak told the Committee, "If children in Texas under the age of 18 cannot consent to sex, then why do they have to prove coercion?"[27] Legislation recommended by the task force would address this problem area in combating human trafficking.

---

[2] H.B. 4009 authorized up to $10 million in grant funding, but the account was not funded.

FEW RESOURCES DEVOTED TO HUMAN TRAFFICKING

In Texas there are some 350 state, county, and local law enforcement agencies; 94 of these are local municipal police departments in cities throughout the state. In addition to these local law enforcement agencies, there are 254 county sheriff departments and in rural areas of the state these are the principal form of police protection. The Texas Ranger Division is the law enforcement agency with statewide jurisdiction.

To facilitate law enforcement against human trafficking, the Justice Department under the TVPA currently funds 42 local law enforcement agencies to combat human trafficking.[28] These task forces bring together resources from the federal, state and local level to investigate all forms of human trafficking. In the State of Texas, there are four federally funded task forces—two at the county level and two at the municipal level. They include:

- Dallas Police Department and Fort Worth Police Department (*in a joint operation*),
- Austin Police Department,
- Bexar County Sheriff's Department,
- Harris County Sheriff's Department.

As part of the grant, there is a requirement to collect and report data on human trafficking.[3] The Justice Department has a program in place for the central management, collection, and reporting of data from the task forces. In the first reporting period, January 1, 2007, through September 30, 2008, task forces nationwide reported the investigation of 1,229 alleged incidents of human trafficking.[29]

In addition to law enforcement efforts, under the condition of these grants recipient agencies are to work cooperatively with local non-governmental agencies that provide rehabilitation assistance to the victims. This initiative is considered a critical component of the program, in part because victim services are a crucial part of the investigation and prosecution of human trafficking cases.

In the Dallas and Fort Worth area, the task force collaborates with Mosaic Services and SafeHaven. In Austin, the police department works with the Central Texas Coalition against Human Trafficking. In Bexar County the Sheriff Department partners with Catholic Charities. In Harris County the Sheriff Department has a collaborative partnership with the YMCA.

> Of the 350 law enforcement agencies in Texas, only 4 have a federally funded task force devoted to fighting human trafficking.

As victims have often suffered extreme physical and mental abuse, persons rescued have a multitude of health needs. There is also a need for temporary lodging that not only meets immediate essential physical needs but is a secure haven from potential violence and retribution by the traffickers. At the federal level there is no funding targeted exclusively for victims of human trafficking; in Texas as well no state funding exists solely to provide services to victims of human trafficking.[30]

---

[3] In addition to the four federally funded task forces in Texas, El Paso also voluntarily reports statistics on human trafficking.

State-wide Initiatives

At the state level, a newly created task force has been put into place to aggressively pursue human traffickers in Texas. The Texas Legislature created the task force last year, calling for the Attorney General's office to oversee a mix of state and local law enforcement officers, state social services personnel, and representatives from various nongovernmental organizations.[31]

While Texas already has four local task forces funded by the Justice Department, the new task force will connect investigations and intelligence throughout the state. The Texas Human Trafficking Prevention Task Force will coordinate, fortify and expand law enforcement tools to prosecute traffickers and help better identify victims. In 2010, the task force held its first meeting at the Texas Summit on the Trafficking and Exploitation of Children, an event organized by Children at Risk.

> **"We are not going to be defeated by human trafficking. It is a horrific crime that affects far too many people."**
> **--Texas Attorney General Greg Abbott**

Texas Attorney General Greg Abbott has publicly spoken on human trafficking and the new state-wide initiative against human trafficking. According to the Attorney General, traffickers have turned Texas into a hub for international and domestic forced labor and prostitution rings. As Attorney General Abbott announced at a press conference, "We are not going to be defeated by human trafficking. It is a horrific crime that affects far too many people."[32]

Harris County

Harris County is in southeastern Texas and is part of the Houston metropolitan area. Houston sits along the I-10 interstate corridor, which has been identified as one of the main routes for human trafficking in the state of Texas.

In 2007, a formal task force, the Human Trafficking Rescue Alliance, was formed with a two-year grant of $450,000 under TVPA from the Justice Department. The new task force funds several full-time deputies to the Harris County Sheriff's Department devoted exclusively to the investigation of human trafficking in the county. The task force is composed of one sergeant, who supervises four investigators.

> **Since 2005 the Houston Task Force has investigated 68 cases of human trafficking and prosecuted 38 cases.**

Harris County was one of the first areas in the country to aggressively pursue human trafficking. Previous to the formation of the formal task force, an informal task force was established in 2005 to combat human trafficking. Known as the Houston Innocence Lost Task Force (HILTF), it was composed of FBI special agents, agents Immigration and Customs Enforcement agents, officers from the vice division of the Houston Police, deputies from the Harris County Sheriff's Office, and other state law enforcement agencies. The collaborative inter-agency approach of HILTF has served as a prototype for other human trafficking law enforcement initiatives to combat human trafficking.[33]

Since the Houston-area task force was first formed in 2005, it has investigated 68 cases of human trafficking, rescued 180 victims, prosecuted 38 defendants, and obtained 31 convictions. A special initiative of the Human Trafficking Rescue Alliance is the proactive location and rescue of children, who are trafficked from the Houston area throughout the state for purposes of commercialized sex.[34]

> **"Public awareness of human trafficking has been raised… but the victims are embedded in communities that are tough to infiltrate. They are hidden in plain sight."**
> *--Sergeant Bruce Carr*

Speaking to the persistent intransigence of the problem, Bruce Carr, sergeant with the Harris County Sheriff's Office, says that there although there is a greater awareness of the problem, investigation and successful prosecution is difficult. "Public awareness of human trafficking has been raised in the last couple of years, but the victims are embedded in communities that are tough to infiltrate. They are hidden in plain sight."[35]

Austin

Austin, the capital city of Texas, has a population of almost one million persons. The Austin City Police Department, in partnership with the Central Texas Coalition against Human Trafficking, has received a grant of $450,000 from the Bureau of Justice Assistance to conduct an anti-human trafficking task force. Similar to the Houston area, the Austin community was actively engaged in anti-trafficking efforts before receiving federal assistance. Under the grant, one detective is funded and assigned full time to investigate human trafficking.

The grant also provides funds for the training of law enforcement officials outside the department. According to Billy J. Sifuentes, liaison to the Human Trafficking Unit, training is vital but some police departments are reluctant to have their officers receive training because it may increase already overwhelming caseloads.

Sifuentes told the Committee: "The biggest challenge in stopping trafficking is the lack of training. Invariably, one or more cases are reported as a result of an officer having received training. However, we continue to struggle with police departments that will not allow training for their officers because the departments feel it may increase caseloads and dip into already limited resources."[36]

> **"The biggest challenge in stopping trafficking is the lack of training. Invariably, one or more cases are reported as a result of an officer having received training."**
> *--Sergeant Billy Sifuentes*

Community mistrust of police agencies also plays a role in impeding efforts to combat human trafficking. Traffickers recognize and exploit this mistrust. Social service agencies therefore play a critical role in combating human trafficking. As Sifuentes told the Texas Advisory Committee: "No law enforcement group can do it alone. The culture of police officers not to be trusted by social workers makes it tough when we speak of the importance of having a non-government coalition to help provide services for victims of trafficking."[37]

Bexar County

Bexar County is in south central Texas and is part of the San Antonio metropolitan area. The total population of the county is almost two million persons. In 2009, the county was awarded a grant of $450,000 from the Justice Department to form a task force to combat human trafficking.

> **Between 2007 and 2009 the Bexar County Task Force reported more than 100 cases of human trafficking.**

The Bexar Sheriff's Department has four deputies serving on its human trafficking task force. A portion of the grant goes to Catholic Charities to provide assistance to victims of human trafficking. Between 2007 and 2009, the task force reported more than 100 cases of human trafficking. [38]

Dallas-Fort Worth

The Dallas-Fort Worth metropolitan area is the fourth largest in the country with a population of over six million people. In 2006 the Dallas and Fort Worth police departments received their first federal grant of $450,000 from the Department of Justice to conduct an anti-human trafficking task force. The task force has continued to receive federal assistance since that time, and in 2010 the task force expanded its operation and re-organized as the North Texas Trafficking Task Force.[39]

The task force operation consists of 18 outside local, state and federal agencies, engaged in both full-time and part-time endeavors with the Dallas and Fort Worth police departments. A key component of this new initiative is intelligence sharing among participating law enforcement agencies. This operational component is viewed as crucial to putting an end to sexual and labor exploitation.[40]

The Dallas-Fort Worth Task Force works in partnership with two non-profit service providers: Mosaic Services in Dallas and SafeHaven in Fort Worth. SafeHaven operates two emergency shelters to assist women and children who have been victims of abuse—including victims of human trafficking. One shelter is in Fort Worth, the other in Arlington.

Mary Lee Hafley, who has worked extensively with victims of human trafficking, said that identifying victims is the greatest obstacle to combating trafficking because victims are so isolated. "[Victims] are most often found through law enforcement entities and brought to shelters like SafeHaven. Otherwise [victims] do not connect to services because they are so completely isolated. Traffickers threaten them, so that the victims believe the fear of what would happen if they leave is greater than the fear of what happens if they stay."[41]

Hafley said the general public tends to think human trafficking as exclusively the sex trade, but there is labor bondage in Texas. One example she shared was about a family from Central America brought to Texas to do farm labor. "Everyone in the family worked, and the sum of all their income was barely at a subsistence level. Another victim is a woman from the United Kingdom, who was trafficked from to Texas to do labor."[42]

CONCLUSIONS

By its very nature, human trafficking is a cruel and vicious practice. Tragically, Texas has emerged as the focal point for this illegal activity. Texas, as one of the largest border states in the United States, is a major destination and transit state for human trafficking. One of every five human trafficking victims has been found enslaved in Texas.

Victims of human trafficking for sexual exploitation have their psyches destroyed and lose their sense of dignity and self worth. Victims of human trafficking for labor exploitation are physically broken, and become powerless to contest the conditions that subjugate them.

Human trafficking is a lucrative enterprise with high-profits and relatively low-risks. With ample supply and growing demand, every year some 1 million to 2 million persons internationally become victims of human trafficking—including thousands here in the United States.

Many social ills such as poverty, homelessness, and broken homes allow human trafficking to exist and thrive. However, human trafficking, does not exist in a vacuum. With one of every five human trafficking victims found enslaved in Texas, clearly many citizens of Texas are engaging the services of these victims.

Moreover, these conditions alone would be insufficient to perpetuate human trafficking without a state of general unawareness by the community. Tragically, to the Texas Advisory Committee, it seems that the citizens of Texas are to a large extent unaware of the magnitude of human trafficking in Texas.

It needs to be understood and acknowledged by the general citizenry that human trafficking—like all civil rights violations—not only scars the victim, but also negatively impacts the community at large. The values and structure of a society are challenged when civil rights violations such as human trafficking are allowed to persist.

Throughout Texas, there are few resources devoted to combating human trafficking. Although there are some 350 local law enforcement agencies in Texas, there are active and engaged anti-human trafficking task forces in just four jurisdictions. In addition to limited law enforcement resources in the state to combat human trafficking, there are few social service agencies equipped to provide treatment for the victims.

There needs to be greater public support for the provision of the necessary resources to adequately investigate and prosecute these crimes. We, as citizens of Texas, should help provide the necessary resources to rehabilitate the victims. This includes support for the efforts of both non-profit organizations as well as churches and ministries that offer rehabilitation services.

With widespread support and resolve, human trafficking in Texas and the United States is a civil rights problem that can be eliminated. We ask the citizens of Texas to become involved and join with the Texas Advisory Committee and others already engaged in combating this violation of fundamental civil rights to do what is necessary to end human trafficking in Texas and in this country.

Endnotes

1. "Over the past 15 years, 'trafficking in persons' or 'human trafficking' have been used as umbrella terms for activities involved when one person obtains or holds another person in compelled service." Trafficking Victims Protection Act, 22 U.S.C. §§ 7101-7112 (2000)(as reauthorized in 2003, 2005, and 2008)(hereafter TVPA).

2. ILO, *A global alliance against forced labor*: 2005 at http://www.ilo.org/wcmsp5/groups/public/@ed_norm/@declaration/documents/publication/wcms_081882.pdf. (hereafter Alliance Against Forced Labor).

3. *Gender and Human Trafficking*, ESCAP, United Nations, at http://www.unescap.org/ESID/GAD/Issues/Trafficking.

4. See *Human Smuggling and Trafficking Center*, Domestic Human Trafficking: An Internal Issue, December 2008, at http://www.state.gov/documents/organization/113612.pdf.

5. United Nations, Global Report on Trafficking, February 2009. http://www.unodc.org/unodc/en/human-trafficking/global-report-on-trafficking-in-persons.html.

6. U.S. Dept. of State, Office to Monitor and Combat Trafficking in Persons, Trafficking in Persons Report, (June 3, 2005).

7. *Modern Slavery*, Civil Rights Issues, U.S. Commission on Civil Rights, June 2001.

8. From presentation to law enforcement officials at U.S. Department of Justice Fourth National Human Trafficking Conference, Atlanta, Ga., September 2008.

9. U.S. Department of Justice, Human Trafficking Data Collection and Reporting Project, *Trafficking in Persons Report*, 2008 (hereafter Trafficking in Persons Report).

10. *Human Trafficking's dirty profits and huge costs*, Inter-American Development Bank, Nov. 2, 2006.

11. *Gender and Human Trafficking*, ESCAP, United Nations, at http://www.unescap.org/ESID/GAD/Issues/Trafficking.

12. *The Texas Response to Human Trafficking*, Health and Human Services Commission Report to the 81st Legis., October 2008, available at http://www.hhsc.state.tx.us/reports/texasresponsehumantrafficking.pdf.

13. Alliance Against Forced Labor.

14. Ibid.

15. Trafficking in Persons Report.

16. *Human Trafficking: The Invisible Slave Trade*, Report of the Houston Rescue and Restore Coalition, April 2007.

17. U.S. Department of Justice, *Report of Activities to Combat Human Trafficking*, 2001-2005, available at http://www.nlpoa.org/US_Department_of_Justice_Report on_Human_Trafficking_Fiscal_Years_2001_2005_NLPOA_1.pdf.

18. Trafficking in Persons Report.

19. 22 U.S.C. §§ 7101-7112 (2000).

20. http://www/fbi/gov/about-us/cjis/ucr/ucr.

21. H.B. 2096.

22. State of Texas, Health and Human Services Commission, Report of the 81st Legislature, *The Texas Response to Human Trafficking*, October 2008 (hereafter Texas Response to Human Trafficking).

23. H.B. 1121 and S.B. 11.

24. H.B. 4009.

25. *Id.*

26. Texas Response to Human Trafficking OAG Report, January 2011, p. 24 (hereafter cites as OAG Human Trafficking Report). Available at https://www.oag.tx/us/ AG_Publications/pdfs/human_trafficking.pdf.

27. Jennifer Solak, Director, Children-at-Risk, Houston, TX, interview, Martha Orozco, Texas Advisory Committee to the U.S. Commission on Civil Rights, Oct. 11, 2010.

28. 22 U.S.C. §§ 7101-7112 (2000).

29. .U.S. Department of Justice, Bureau of Justice Statistics, Human Trafficking. By agreement, the Texas Attorney General has access to data developed by the Human Trafficking Reporting System, funded by the U.S. Department of Justice. See http://bjs.ojp.usdoj.gov/index.cfm?ty=dcdetail&iid=343.

30. Texas Response to Human Trafficking , p. 43.

31. H.B. 4009.

32.

33. Texas Advisory Committee to the U.S. Commission on Civil Rights from information provided by the Human Trafficking Rescue Alliance.

34. Bruce Carr, Harris County Sheriff Office, Interview, Martha Orozco, Texas Advisory Committee to the U.S. Commission on Civil Rights, Dec. 17, 2010.

35. Ibid.

36. Billy J. Sifuentes, Liaison to Austin Police Department, Interview, Barbara Walters, Texas Advisory Committee to the U.S. Commission on Civil Rights, Dec. 17, 2010.

37. Ibid.

38. Texas Advisory Committee to the U.S. Commission on Civil Rights from information provided by the Bexar County Human Trafficking task force.

39. Texas Advisory Committee to the U.S. Commission on Civil Rights from information provided by the North Texas Trafficking Task Force.

40. OAG Human Trafficking Report.

41. Mary Lee Hafley, CEO SafeHaven of Tarrant County, Interview, Barbara Walters, Texas Advisory Committee to the U.S. Commission on Civil Rights, Dec. 17, 2010.

42. Ibid.

Texas Advisory Committee to the

U. S. Commission on Civil Rights

U.S. Commission Contact

USCCR Contact	Peter Minarik, Ph.D.
	Designated Federal Official
	Western Regional Office
	U.S. Commission on Civil Rights
	(213) 894-3437 or pminarik@usccr.gov

Contributors—This report was researched and written by Peter Minarik, Regional Director, Western Region, U.S. Commission on Civil Rights in consultation with the members of the Texas Advisory Committee sub-Committee on Human Trafficking. Hamida Labi provided research support and assisted in the writing of the report.